WINDOW TO THE WORLD

RAJSHREE DIYA

Contents

Contents

Contents

Contents

Contents

END

Preface

A new phase of my life, learning to be more independent and adulting while holding my child-like slef close to me. Capturing moments, dialogues, imaginations, secrets and memories into words never fails to amaze me.

Acknowledgements

Written in the comforts of my room and surrounding, words play an integral part and it wouldn't been completed without the support of my close ones. My parents have supported me enormously throughout the drafting process.

I would like to thank my friends, Parvati, Ananya, Sinchana, Sarayu, Kausani and Rahul for reading, supporting and giving positive criticisms in my works.

Prologue

Dusted books and unopened letters
　　Poetry with vivid filters of sky blue.
　　Trapped, erased and lost
　　Walls with a greyscale,
　　Hide my existence.
　　Room with a view
　　Masking my silence.
　　Moon in the blackout midnight
　　And far away fireflies.
　　Breathe silent lies
　　On my face like my past.
　　As I seek permission
　　From my intelligence
　　To delete the codes and characters
　　Interpretation of future self
　　Awake like a game.
　　I stand vulnerable to the evidence
　　With the temperature of venus.
　　As I look at my life
　　From the concert stage
　　The mirage of the hiraeth
　　And the safety it provides.
　　With butterflies in my stomach
　　And coffee to reboot my mind.

Run away to the **train station**

To reach a new **city**

To the next **chapter** of my life.

POEMS

Adventure Riddles Mystery Magic
Knowledge Rhymes Knowledge
Knowledge Growth Inspiration
Imagination Learning Mystery Growth
Insights Learning
Inspiration Brilliant Thoughts Adventure
HIGGINBOTHAMS

1. VENUS

How can I trust this?
'Safe' wasn't ready.
It was infact killing me.
What if I am wrong?
I'll never know.
What if I never tell?
It'll never leave.
But what to do,
it's bound to my freedom
that I cannot say.
Free me; save me
I'll speak up in solidarity.
You will never know.
if I am hiding my say,
maybe that's what emotions convey?

2. HIDE

Should I say it?
it's a secret hidden for long
of what they are.
I'll mask it under my words,
butterflies will never deny.
Eager to say,
something is holding me back.
Is it the emptiness of revealing the truth?

3. EXISTENCE

When I travel away,
will I know where I am going?
Is this all a lucid dream?
Would I know when it's over?
The ground will disappear,
so will this frame.
But what if it all boils down
to identity and name?
This gold and embroidery,
worth the luxury,
really matter?
I am not carrying it neither are my queries.
Just memories and that's it.
But wait,
will I remember them?

4. HIRAETH

Never thought of losing you
what if it all goes away,
this mess and the restless.
Someday I have to.
Is it all fading,
of the things I conceptualised.
Will it be the end,
of what I wish to see
and whether was it all worth
to let it go in the end.
It will all come to this goodbye,
which is not right.
How will I face myself
to the mirrors that reflect everything I know
but would I be able to write
I wouldn't know.

5. CHARACTERS

I wonder who will get what
these characters portray
our lives to a point.
We'll fall in a world
of what if and why.
and change the written narration
like how colours collide.
Comfort these lines
and tell me your lies,
I can see what you hide.
For I am real,
tell me what you find.

6. DUSTED BOOKS

• 10 •

Books dusted in fingertips
of those who once touched them
and left their memories for a stranger.
These hands they touch forever
from strangers to things alike
but do these hands recognise
the other end
and feel the same
from their own point?

7. UNOPENED LETTERS

Subtle dark to these horizon lights
will flood in colours of the world that never saw.
Why should we wait till the day gets dark,
only to reveal the letters we never opened?

8. POETRY

Make it vulnerable,
all that exists is beauty.
This fragile blood flows freely
for that it all bleeds in silent words
of feelings that are well hidden in poetry.
Who art thou, so wise,
shall seek the truth.
Like wilted flowers.
holding shape yet bent.
Bloated pages will soak all in
stained sheets will give it back.
Would the ink wither away
when we all go away?

9. VIVID FILTERS

All the things I reflected on,
are there in front of this glass.
Where did all the vivid filters go,
that these eyes fail to see.
My eyes keep fooling me,
where do I seek
Are you right behind me?
this hide and seek.
Wonder where it all stays
towers dipping from endless heights.
You ran away-
my characters will say. Wait-
Why did you return
when you left me in the first place?

10. FIREFLIES

• 14 •

Is it illusion,
to see a million lights
flooding in the dark night
and wondering why do they live
with such a short life?
I guess that's nature.
Who are we to decide?
The fire will fly
igniting the light
like stars
of nothing else but life.

11. TRAIN STATION

Silence prevailed over these seats
as the sun set movingly.
Announce the stop
the passengers get off.
An undefined object
to an unknown eye
shall not know the worth
to the eyes that leave memories behind.

12. GREYSCALE

A world without colours,
among the premise
characters will show
the trail they left behind.
Plot against the empty land
the surprise element shall rise
would this theme ever be alive?

13. LOST

Strike me hard
so much I can forget.
What did I do,
pondered the thought.
Reach out for the material
to jot these questions.
Desperate-a pen
give me something!
Too late or goodbye
each is one of a kind.
Do return back
"Sorry what happened?"-zoned out.

14. LIE

What if we both are lying
through the eyes
that slide away.
Should I have revealed the truth,
how can I,
the numbers play the game
and all exists a lie.

15. STAGE

For all the world's a stage.
Cue the spotlight.
on these stages
I'll write my play.
Slipped paper will tumble down
like ruins of another life.
Should I go above my head,
and think majestic?
That these stairs are a throne,
ranking my words
from high to low?

16. TRAPPED

Should it surrender the gap,
for all the meanings that were borrowed.
Answer by the call,
hide the truth in the wall
who will break the cement sleet
and damage the perfect wall?
Decipher; cross question
what do I really mean?
Define art-is it really a mystery?
Overshoot my limit
would I be caught for my art?

17. ROOM

Lonely roads would find itself,
deprived of connection.
Why does it take a festival
to bring everything to life,
where else the city plunges
into the monotonous life?
Stitch it up like a tailored wall
throw out of the comfort sight.
Dark night with street lights
shall hypnotise these fickle eyes.
And stare into the distance,
just wavy coloured lights.
There is no shelter above
or a net below
Suspended.
Fear stricken in these eyes
the sky stands before.

18. POWER CUT

Bring out the darkness
to hide amongst the universe.
Who will find
what are you,
just an atom.
The world will fall silent,
eagle angle on cities
that will plunge into the void.
In the spotlight of the blackout
and just the same like
we become anonymous.

19. ERASED

My boards have been erased
of all the things I wrote.
Drafts have been replaced
by unknown words.
Time has gotten away,
like a lost friend.
What if I lose it all,
all these thoughts
and all this mess.
Is it all worth,
I wouldn't know.
Safe with a back up plan,
catch me if you can.

20. MIRAGE

• 24 •

Seemingly merge among these roads,
and showcase the display of an imagery.
To what extent will you remember the details?
What is the illusion you portray,
in reality or just a vivid virtuality
of whether you were really there?

21. EVIDENCE

• 25 •

Playing powder dusted on my hands
Just like how cloud mist traces
On the craters of the moon
Does it wish to wash away?
Like my hands wishes water
And remove evidence
Of the imprints I left behind.

22. GAME

Flower postcards on the counter top
and prints on the wall
clues left behind
for the world to find.
Seep in the fantasy
that make your drink.
For who will question
on your liking
red-white, strong or light?
Ruse,
how can I capture colours
from the sky and land it on my walls
drunk in its original form.
Did I tell about my escape plan
or trick into believing one?

23. CONCERT

As I view the fading sunset
from the room that echoes my laughter.
An unrequited sadness prevails
questioning- that's it?
All waited for is over.
The strobe coloured stages
a million mesmerised eyes.
The sound of hidden emotions
keep playing in that light.
Time flew too fast-
and in that time, the world stood still.
Lost away in their thoughts-
thinking about who, what and why.
Recorded from my lenses
about the moments that went away.
Not a long ago,
leaves me with an afterthought.
About the things I felt at that time
slowly it slips into another memory of mine.

24. PAST

Is this the thrill I always missed
to see the world from a map point.
Leave a thousand memories behind.
didn't even get a chance to say goodbye.
Torn contacts and dreams
will never see faces again.
Would all our fate change,
as our life progresses.
And one day we'll meet on the streets
all the lives that knew once
would either coincide or be left behind.

25. WALLS

I don't want a room with no thoughts
that would stare with its blank walls.
Pale shadows traverse through windows
grilled in silver white bars.
City hunted curtains and teak wood stands
compliments on the prints, quotes and lights
"Nice! Pretty!" is everyone's say.
Bring in some questions
let the walls be a mess.
Copper lights provide- warmth
the sleepless night recalls.
Fallout like autumn leaves
and whitewash the canvas.
Now I stand again with my memories
in a room with no thoughts.

26. FUTURE SELF

• 30 •

I have left hints for you to hunt,
not to me, but to a place
where you can,
write and design, laugh and cry,
in the memory of mine.

27. FAR AWAY

A far away land
is emerging among our senses.
Would we all be alive
to find what it truly holds
and all the things
this world is too afraid to show.
Is it us?

28. SAFETY

How can I judge so soon,
not reached the half mile.
Leave in safe hands
faces that are hidden.
They fear the same thing.
Out on the streets
with connections on the tips,
toning the voices
telling what the danger is.
Left vulnerable to return back
across the city with traffic times.
Exposed can be said,
how sure am I that
this target is not meant for mine?

29. COFFEE

Coffee pages fall so free
amidst the dark background
that falls to my feet.
Inspect the blank sheets
as though stories were written in discreet.
And in order to stain the sheets
with the smell of heavy words
in shades of brown.
Had to get my hands coloured
in patches- an uneven work.
Like how some parts of this
story that went missing.

30. RUN AWAY

Stained glass colours
will reduce patterns that languages never spoke.
A million rooms with a single view
to the world of a thousand lives.
Who will show the door way out,
titles are placed everywhere.
Haunted by the windows
caught up in this blueprint maze.
What am I alive for
Just to breathe and sometimes lie?
Some of us are missing
could this be a new night?
Run away in to the centre
window to the world shall be route.
Keys will deny access
in order to never return back.

31. VULNERABLE

Vulnerable to sharing
I'll hide it all away,
even my eyes won't lie.
Embedded deep
fearing what the world might.
Shadows trails on these walls,
as the nights leave me awake.
I'll question why this
couldn't it have been something else?
The records will never capture
and the dates would fade.
Did I lose,
or have I given it all away?
The hints are calling
I shall wound.
Free falling
let me go.

32. CODE

Creative enough
to cypher these words.
Let them wonder
what you know.
Interpretation of many
many means that of course,
the background; the tone.
But how cold?
Who else would know
what is jotted down
in order to hide your secrets
from the world?
What if you didn't hide them,
rather remember them,
in encryption code.

33. MASK

I'll mask it under my skin,
can't guarantee that my body will hide.
About the things I want to let go
maybe it never meant to.
Goodbye is what I didn't ask
yet I'll be silent for sake
I wonder who will find
if it all be said, say it now.
So much could have been said,
but here, sit in vain.
If all of this vanishes away,
would you remember what you said?

34. BREATHE

• 38 •

Strive to breath in between the lines
and take a pause.
To the end of the line,
running out of things to say.
So outdone,
the pens are still new.
Listen, it's hard
to deal with words.
But who am I without these names
nothing but just-
the flaw is broken.
Am I just spitting out words-
words that sound high pitched.
No space left to breathe.

35. FACE

• 39 •

Scars and marks

on this combination.

Uneven tail ends- one spilt two.

Mismatched lines

small patch engulfs the corner,

but what about these eyes?

Too painful to touch

the silent speak.

What do you really know about me?

What haven't I seen?- they ask.

Mirrors are all I see,

could be something I missed.

Maybe, you are stuck inside.

I know that secret of yours- they whispered at the back of my

mind.

36. MOON

Paint a clear picture
as this night falls
on the bed as I lay down.
"I wish we could date the sky, the stars"
-my friend narrated once.
What brings the world to sleep in,
when all of us are hidden.
Where else would we go,
if not where we live now.
Would it all matter-
did I think too much?
Maybe that's why the world is restless
and the moon was there before my eyes
and left without saying goodbye.

37. TEMPERATURE

• 41 •

I hold things down,
the way my heart sank to my stomach.
For that the fall was new.
Nails turned into a sunset
of pink, periwinkle and pale.
Trickled to the ending tips,
that stood stiff like the winter's breeze.
Too stoned to touch, but warm blood flowed.
The feet wrapped in grey wool
numb to the hard cold marble floor.
And my hands were too frozen,
for the words to be written,
froze in my silence.

38. SKY BLUE

These hands my dear
have fallen weak.
Weak, where recognition
is not in sight.
Sight. These eyes have seen,
them work a million times.
Now they have fallen blue
like these hands,
That sculpted the blue sky
for these eyes to see.

39. MIDNIGHT

Equidistant parallel curtains,
except the sheer- blur the glass
so that shadows play on the walls
reflecting the aesthetic lines.
Does the wall seem a bit tilted to you?
Blood rush to the head.
Intrinsic and intriguing lie beside
on this bed made of poetry.
For your amazement: I am still awake
in the unearthly hours
when the world falls asleep.
Exempting those on the road
taking diversions,
while I create my own.

40. INTELLIGENCE

While hiding the secret
or to fill up the reader's shelves.
But what would it mean to me?
Soon, the answer is out in the open.
Open in the cerebral time and minds.
What's next for me to search,
is it a test of intelligence?

41. REBOOT

• 45 •

Memory overload,
for you to make me a dream.
A dream counting,
of the activities-real or not.
Jolt me before I restfully lay,
remove the bed below me.
What are you proving to me,
or-
Are you erasing my memory?

42. SILENCE

All gone too far,
the city haunted
of evidence falling like rain.
Wish to burn it off
five levels high
the candle flickered
but no wind from any corner.
Eyes are bagged
and some are missing
nothing more to offer.
Error-
destination has arrived,
in front of the knowledge centre
but the city remain silent
in a plague with no answer.

43. INTERPRETATION

Out of silence
the records fail.
Interpretations float around
losing the source trail.
Who wrote the real phrase,
neither you nor me.
"Leave it to the imagination"- they say
Correct in a way
but how true to an artist's taste?
Of what they felt
and what's the way.
Each on their own
narrating a different say.

44. BUTTEFLIES

• 48 •

Wish to write things
I could never say.
I'll leave off on the table
double dot and a curve.
Telepathy maybe a way
but this ain't a science fiction
To let another imagine the pain.
Pain, to have butterflies,
and my clothes hide the knot.
I escaped the confession,
but the butterflies rot.

45. SILENT

The fears lines up next
as these drafts stay idle,
and my quest stays silent.
What if these aesthetics die down
burning pages of unspoken truth,
would it erase the pain?
The sky is on fire.
Maybe one day it'll fly away
these eyes are scared to sleep.

46. CITY

Double than eight to travel
and could say it's not tiring.
Skies changing moods on their canvas.
and roads falling under- unknown names.
Buildings bring me back to,
smell the heaviness of words
as rain drops in the golden liquid.
Canopies shading the sliver sunlight
light up the scenic sight.
Another city in this boundary lines.
Lose enough to find a say,
came out from this closed space.
"This city has treated you well"
-my friend said.

47. DELETE

Do I dare to delete,
ink smudged in my drafts
I said what,
no dates have been recorded.
And some stay immature.
Mind playing games.
Interpretation twisted,
like a two way mirror face.
Just like my age.
There it's gone.
Everything I had known.
But why do I fallback upon,
bringing the words that no longer mean to me?

48. AWAKE

Still hidden
in the dark corners of this room.
Waiting for your arrival.
I'll slip into these sheets soon.
Where did you go,
today it's my turn.
Anything for you to say?
"Yesterday's draft was great"
Midnight blues,
and no thoughts
maybe, today I won't get to hear
your voice in my mind.

49. PERMISSION

Do I have your permissions in my draft?
Too soon did I ask,
after writing a century of titles and words.
Where do you lie among here,
the secret is safe.
But do the world know,
that I am letting you escape,
of what you have locked in.
Let them guess,
how you have been a part
and let them catch you
but do you really exist in their minds?

50. CHAPTER

Stop. Still. Quiet.
The clouds caress across the sky,
the flowers sway in roots.
Colours stripped naked,
curtains fall aloof.
And these eyes,
wide awake
beholding thousand secrets.
For months I have been silent,
to hide this work from the outside.
Written thousand, repaired millions.
Showed the range of emotions,
written in my room.
Would you take a look into my dream?
Rather my world?

MEANINGS

51. Venus

• 59 •

When you hide an unknown secret, and the butterflies in the stomach yearn to be released but you have no idea who to reveal it to. Whom do you trust? Does body language and emotions convey the things you aren't able to say?

52. Hide

When you wish to utter the truth because you cannot hold it back anymore, but your conscience keeps pulling you back. A struggle whether to hide it or say it, what do you do? How do you escape?

53. Existence

When we all shall leave this planet, what do we really carry with ourselves? Do we even know where we are even going? Would we even take all the possessions like gold and all the luxury or even remember ourselves- name, identity or even our memories?

54. Hiraeth

Hiraeth means homesickness for a home you can't return to or that never was.

This poem is in context to what if I never wrote. That thought led me to write this poem. It's a pondering thought to question.

What if one day, I lose all my interest and feelings towards writing. Then what? How can I let go of something that has made me who I am now. Maybe that's what everything is: to let go at some point.

55. Characters

When I began writing short fictions a few years ago, when it came to character basis, I always picked up the personality of my characters from my known ones: be it my friends, parents or even me. And how amazing it is to create a character who can have a mix of two personalities.

56. Dusted books

• 64 •

So, basically two things. Hands and library. Library where a million words and pages are stacked and for some reason, the dust that settles on them shows a unique gesture. How the book occupy the space while the place around has traces of dust. And how people have come to these places for escaping, reading, exploring and as they touch the books, they leave an impression of themselves on these books. Expect the idea of touch, do our own hands know the other one?

57. Unopened letters

When the night comes, some sleep and some don't. What if we are missing a different world altogether? And why do we hide among the night, just to reveal things that we are too afraid to tell?

58. Poetry

The idea of writing poems, to be able to write feelings and emotions in a verse that has many meanings. Basically, the ink is the blood that flows in the papers and that voices are silent yet present. A plethora of works present and more to come. But, who will go to the extent to find what it all means, the truth? And what if, the ink that contains our words slowly fades away like how with time, we also fade, becoming a memory?

59. Vivid Filters

These eyes have seen the world and are the source to view, but why did our childhood days seem more vivid than our teenage years? Is it life?

60. Fireflies

• 68 •

When monsoon hits the skies and evenings are filled with the expectation of fireflies throughout the house so you plan to sit in the silence of the dark with a small ray of the light penetrating through the glass window. And wondering why such subtle creatures of life have such a short lifespan.

61. Train Station

Travelling in the metro has always given a sort of peace and comfort. This was written a few days before I left for my colleg,e which is in another city. It made me wonder that I am leaving everything I know here.

62. Greyscale

On a sprint project my friends and I did on, that too under ten minutes, we captured a series of black and white images and narrated a storyline of our own. We narrated how once the streets and places were empty (during the times of the pandemic), how people left their trail or footsteps behind and questioning would the silence ever be alive for that life is on the new normal.

63. Lost

• 71 •

Even statements make a lot of sense to me, and during lectures, converstaions I start analysing things people say and would make me write something on that spot. And if I don't write at that moment, the thought I had would vanish like a blink of an eye. And in that whole process I would zone out not knowing what is going on around me.

64. Lie

• 72 •

When you hide the truth from your known ones and the guilt that rises only because you can't utter out and even if you do, you start to wonder the consequences the situation presents. Everyone hides something about the others that they do not wish to find out.

65. Stage

Standing at the majestic stairs of a place I visit regularly, waiting for my friend. I had a vague thought of throwing all my written drafts down the stairs. It seemed pretty obscure first because I was aiming at the aesthetic sense it will give. But what if these stairs narrate or criticise my works indirectly?

66. Trapped

• 74 •

A small tribute to the artists, writers, composers and individuals who were caught for making their masterpiece/art and had to publish works/pieces that played safe.

67. Room

My rooms has sheer cream curtains through which light passes subtly in the night and the shadows it leaves on the walls feels like the walls have the look of the wall being tailored. And the warm colours of the sunsets that falls in the room is a sense of warmth and mesmerising.

68. Power Cut

A piece inspired when I went to a resturant with my family for dinner. We sat in the open sky, as I counted the countless stars hinted with the subtle lights the resturant and the neighbouring places had. And all of a sudden was a blackout/ power cut. And in those ten minutes of utter darkness, it struck to me, that we all are/were anonymous in that moment where I was transported to my childhood of visiting a planetorium- no light, just darkness and here we are among a million others.

69. Erased

• 77 •

A moment where I started erasing my writing drafts to acccompany my academic notes on my whiteboard, which were written in a neat and orderly fashion. Not complaining, but I did miss the mess I had created with my drafts. And I wondered if I would lose the mess and drafts?

70. Mirage

• 78 •

When we narrate an incident or our daily life, we tend to either miss out details or bring in changes to the story. What is real and what is not?

71. Evidence

After a smashing game of carrom board and on my way home, we stopped at the terrace of our apartment, to view the city, the stars and the moon. My hands were covered in the carrom powder and the eagerness I have to wash it off because it's dust and I would touch my face unknowingly. And I wondered, 'what about the moon, that has evidences of footsteps, rovers and shuttles, on it's dusted craters?'

72. Game

The genre of mystery/Thriller books, movies and games are the series that I have been watching since a kid. So much so, certain plots have helped in some of my other written works. It's quite fascinating how a interwoven plot is laid in a complex yet in a manner where everything connects. And the idea of escape rooms, have always delighted me as this is the only game I haven't played and maybe one day I can get to.

73. Concert

Written in the aftermath of a concert I attended virtually on 28th December 2021. This was the first concert ever attending; the excitement was at peak throughout the year. And as the day arrived, the concert took place in the four walls of my room accompanied by a gradient sunset and laughter where it all became a reality.

74. Past

Always had a thought of what if I meet my long-lost friends on the streets (of any city) and would I be able to recognise them?

75. Walls

The idea strikes of how we decorate our respectively room walls with posters, art, clippings, equations, notes, photos and even writings. Moreover, the thought of getting more things stuck on the wall. What happens to those when you shift from that place, do they get washed away and would be able to think that this was your room before?

76. Future Self

•

As a kid, I used to collect items that meant a lot to me and keep it in my memory box, so I could come back later and reminiscence. Or in other words, I was making a place (and still) for my future self to come back and visit the childhood and think how different I was, what all things felt dear to me. On what it feels like to be a kid again.

77. Far Away

With all the new studies of showing life in other planets or so, I wonder if we all would be awake to see the magic and miracles it brings. Moreover, is it because of us, that we are in search for another platform that supports life?

78. Safety

With all the travelling during these pandemic times and everyone I know being worried about getting exposed is very evident in their tones. And how sure are we, that all the precautions we take are enough? Or how sure are we that we won't be a target?

79. Coffee

I still remember staining printing paper with a mixture of holt water and instant coffee to give it an old and antique look where later on I would write letters or do calligraphy. I would stain the sheets on the granite counter and after a while the whole area smelled like coffee. And the residue it leaves on the small patches in the corner of the paper is what I loved the most. Most of all, my hands would turn brown and smell like coffee residue. And some patches would be dry.

And this let me correlate on how some pieces of works remain incomplete because the page would have been torn or the left unattented, because of not giving it that much importance or just ran out of ideas like how I would run out of the coffee mixture.

80. Run away

Basically what are we alive for? Just to exist, breathe, study, earn and live a life? Could there be something more than we are acustomed to? Shall we all run to a place where things make sense and to find what life living really means?

81. Vulnerable

Being vulnerable to things are quite a strong guard we hold to. And the overwhelming fear of not knowing how to tell someone is quite a challenge. And these leave one awake for a night or two and the constant doubt or fear of telling more than you "should" have and the idea of providing hints. So much so, that you try to run away from yourself not knowing your shadow is trailing behind you.

82. Code

• 90 •

Taking inspiration from the Enigma Variations by Edward Elgar, what if the things we write, compose, paint, sculpt, are sort of a code that has our deepest secret interwoven in it, that makes it stand out on the surface of the eyes of others but holds something raw inside?

83. Mask

• 91 •

How we conceal things from uttering yet our body langauge, face and emotions depict everything? And the statement we make to assure that we are fine.

84. Breathe

In the process of writing this work, there were times, when I couldn't write for days and weeks and the pens would stay idle. No idea or thought came to my mind for me to write and I let that be. I would get a bit flustered that no drafts were being written but I trusted the writing process and hence, breathe.

85. Face

• 93 •

What if all the secrets you know in the back of your mind but you tend to forget them, but your eyes speak out?

86. Moon

Space has quite interested me over the years, and no matter
how many times one views the moon, the sight always leaves
a different imprint of memory than the previous one. Songs,
poems, classical music, stories and other forms of creativity
have captured the essence of the moon in it's eyes. And yet, it's
always eternal to look at.

87. Temperature

In the winter seasons, my hands and legs would turn cold and discoloured and the cold feeling would leave me confused because there are so much that I want to write but my hands would go stiff and painful. How should I write then?

88. Sky blue

• 96 •

A piece written from the corners of my room as I was mesmerised by the rich blue sky captured in my windows and it felt like the sky was sculpted by hands for the eyes to see.

89. Midnight

Written on a midnight, when I kept staring at the walls as I couldn't sleep and watched the so called 'night-life'. I lay on my bed which is made of poems and my creativity as I could hear the cars and bike riders on the road taking their own path, while I was creating my own.

90. Intelligence

• 98 •

A piece inspired from one of the courses on artificial intelligence I was studying on. The saying goes along the lines of intelligence is the quest for an answer you don't know to the next question. And the sense of getting to know the answer is satisfaction but the quest to find the answer must continue.

91. Reboot

When our daily life happening moments gets interwoven in our dreams; and the moments when you start to fall asleep but you start dreaming things that do not make sense. And the feeling that you're falling is what wakes you up, leaving you confused.

92. Silence

To the trips I have taken to my favourite bookstore in the city during the peak times of the pandemic, the streets would be so empty and dull, giving the city a haunted feeling. The long journey to the centre of the city would take me around an hour to travel but with the empty streets, it felt like just ten minutes. How does time run so fast, that you aren't even aware?

93. Interpretation

Interpretation of anything could be seen in many ways and it's to each individual's perspective. But some intepretations get lost over the time; we still do not know that the things we know are true or not and whether if those meanings are really what they (for example author or poet) wanted us to interpret.

94. Butterflies

The feeling of having something to say- a thought, feeling or a confession which keeps one up at night. And the Butterflies in the stomach feeling creating a knot and clothes have the power to hide this "knot". But it's evident how it controls one- the rage and the wish to speak out.

And what if one escaped from uttering that thought; be it different scenarios yet knowing what's going on and not knowing that the knot or the butterflies remain inside, degrading that feeling overtime.

95. Silent

The fear (and somewhat similar to the poem HIRAETH) is what if I stop finding things that make me write? What if my quest to search for emotions and specifically the hidden ones goes down? Then what? Where would my words exist and at what basis?

96. City

A few months into the city and for sure I have fallen in love here. A city not new to my eyes, for sure has shown me it's real beauty. Standing at a higher altitude, the sky shows its colours at times with the sound of the helicopter blades. Rain is the guest that arrives at any time without prior notice. The strange weather of this city, keeps shifting between the cold, hot and lazy London temperatures. And the city leaves no dearth when it comes to festivals. '*Leave before the traffic time*' is every Bangalorean's statement.

The trips to the college everyday begins with the question of which route the auto guy will take: the Kodihalli-Domlur-Ejipura or the Banaswadi-Ulsoor-Trinity route. And to travel 18 kilometres, plus the subtle 'thank you', I reply after they leave me at my destination. Communicating in Tamil and English while still trying to speak Kannda (since I understand).

How can I forget the sulk of walking the skywalk to cross the road to enter the college campus along with 15 more minutes to get to my block. And the ID card that hangs around my neck, each day reminds me that it's finally college. But at the campus, the world seem different. The ecology, people and the energy, each holding different stories and emotions. Numerous canteens, two basketball courts and two libraries are enough to spend time during our regular class schedules. The scenery at the top of the central building, captures all of Bengaluru in it's windows. And the famous UB tower tells me, how much I travel from home to campus. Travelling back home in the metro lets me skip the loud traffic and view the city from a better height with the peace that I love. And in between lies my favourite Blossoms bookstore where I spend three hours finding all the books I wrote on a piece of paper or look for postcards, that is adjacent to café Matteo on Church Street that makes coffee as strong and bitter as I like with blueberry danish that is pure bliss.

This city has given everything I need, a safe space, confidence, the wish to explore more and to meet people.

Each day spark inspirations for my writings accompanied by the stars at night. And each night I go to bed, wondering what magic this city will show me the next day.

97. Delete

My notebooks and phone notes have innumerable drafts or notes that I write whenever inspiration or candid lines spark. Certainly, I wish to use in my future works. But at times, when I do come back and read them, I tend to delete them thinking that I wouldn't be needing it because I wouldn't connect to what I wrote. And after a while of contemplation I would restore the deleted draft, hoping it would be useful again.

98. Awake

Sub-conscious productivity arises in the night time, personally and I can't help how annoying it is (even though it helps me write drafts) because I get thoughts the moment I am about to fall asleep. So the sulk of getting up to find my phone and write the spontaneous thoughts is quite a challenge.
But some nights when I await for my thoughts to arise, I get nothing. Not forcing to write is something I have learnt well and I'll leave off for the day.

99. Permission

• 108 •

Permission or consent. Most of my drafts incorporate the feelings and confession my friends have told me. And I use their experiences in words to speak out. But, did I do the right thing?

100. Chapter

Each individual have different chapters at different point in life and here is mine for the writing period of this work where I found sources around me and integrated with stories I know and heard.

END

www.ingramcontent.com/pod-product-compliance
Lightning Source LLC
Chambersburg PA
CBHW020726160726